JENTEZEN

Why Bless Israel

A Biblical Call To Bless Israel
& How It Impacts Your Life

Why Bless Israel: A Biblical Call to Bless Israel & How It Impacts Your Life

Copyright © 2024 Jentezen Franklin Media Ministries

All rights reserved. No part of this book may be reproduced or transmitted in any form or by any means, electronic or mechanical, including photocopying, recording, or by any information storage and retrieval system, without permission in writing from the publisher.

Scripture quotations marked ESV are taken from The ESV® Bible (The Holy Bible, English Standard Version®), © 2001 by Crossway, a publishing ministry of Good News Publishers. All rights reserved.

Scripture quotations marked NASB are taken from the (NASB®) New American Standard Bible®, Copyright © 1960, 1971, 1977, 1995, 2020 by The Lockman Foundation. Used by permission. All rights reserved. lockman.org

Scripture quotations marked NIV are taken from the Holy Bible, New International Version®, NIV®. Copyright © 1973, 1978, 1984, 2011 by Biblica, Inc.™ Used by permission of Zondervan. All rights reserved worldwide. www.zondervan.com The "NIV" and "New International Version" are trademarks registered in the United States Patent and Trademark Office by Biblica, Inc.™

Scripture quotations marked NKJV are taken from the New King James Version®. Copyright © 1982 by Thomas Nelson. Used by permission. All rights reserved.

ISBN: 978-1-963492-20-0

Assembled and Produced for Jentezen Franklin Media Ministries by
Breakfast for Seven
breakfastforseven.com

Printed in the United States of America.

Now the LORD **had said to Abram: "Get out of your country, from your family and from your father's house, to a land that I will show you.** I will make you a great nation; I will bless you and make your name great; and you shall be a blessing. I will bless those who bless you, and I will curse him who curses you; and in you all the families of the earth shall be blessed."

Genesis 12:1–3 (NKJV)

"I will establish My covenant between Me and you and your descendants after you in their generations, for an everlasting covenant, to be God to you and your descendants after you. Also I give to you and your descendants after you the land in which you are a stranger, all the land of Canaan, as an everlasting possession; and I will be their God."

Genesis 17:7–8 (NKJV)

Table of Contents

Introduction vii

A Biblical Principle

  1 In Blessing I Will Bless You 1
  2 A Divine Plan 9
  3 The Firstfruits are Holy 13
  4 Zealous for Zion 23

Everlasting Covenants

  5 An Established Covenant 35
  6 The Apple of His Eye 43
  7 Israel in Prophecy 49
  8 A People, a Land, a Covenant 57

Faith in Action

  9 Pray for the Peace of Jerusalem 67
  10 Holy to the Lord 75
  11 I Will Not Forget You 85
  12 Watchmen on the Wall 93

Key Verses Concerning Israel 101
My Pledge 106

Introduction

We're living in extraordinary days. Exciting days in many respects. But troubling ones, as well. One of the most disturbing trends emerging over the last few years is the way open hatred of Israel and the Jewish people in general has become not only visible but acceptable in many quarters.

Even many Christians seem confused about why they should esteem the miraculous little nation that, in 1948, became an island of modernity and Western values in a hostile sea of Islamic culture. Too many believers don't understand the biblical case for Israel's importance and role in God's good plans for mankind. This little book was created to provide sound, scriptural answers to those questions.

You see, there are more than 2,000 verses in the Bible that refer to Israel, the Jewish people, or Jerusalem. Israel is mentioned so many times throughout the Bible that you can flip open your Bible at random and most likely find a reference to Israel on any given page.

Israel is found throughout the Bible, from Genesis to Revelation and, still today, Israel is important to God. The Bible says that God never changes. He is the same yesterday, today, and forever (Hebrews 13:8). He cared about Israel in the Old Testament, He cared about Israel in the New Testament, and He cares about Israel today.

The fact is, Israel—as a nation and a people—has always been part of God's plan to reveal Himself to the world. His ways are greater than ours, and His plans are grander than we can comprehend. And there is an eternal biblical principle that activates in your life when you honor it. That principle is:

When you bless Israel, there is a blessing that comes on your life.

In Genesis 12, God spoke to Abraham, saying:

> *"Get out of your country, from your family and from your father's house, to a land that I will show you. I will make you a great nation;* ***I will bless you and make your name***

great; and you shall be a blessing. I will bless those who bless you, and I will curse him who curses you; and in you all the families of the earth shall be blessed."
(Genesis 12:1–3, NKJV, emphasis added)

In the chapters that follow, we'll see that Abraham ultimately became the father of the 12 tribes of Israel through his grandson, Jacob. A few thousand years after that Genesis 12 promise of blessing, Paul wrote something similar in his letter to the church at Rome—he was on his way to Jerusalem in service of the Lord's people and wanted to bring a contribution for the poor there. He wrote about the believers' gifts from Macedonia and Achaia who gave to help them.

He wrote: *"They were pleased to do it, and indeed they owe it to them. For if the Gentiles have shared in the Jews' spiritual blessings, they owe it to the Jews to share with them their material blessings"* (Romans 15:27, NIV).

Whether we recognize it or not, all believers have shared in the spiritual blessings of Israel. God gave much through the Jewish people. Romans 9:4 says of them, *"... who are Israelites, to whom pertain the adoption, the glory, the covenants, the giving of the law, the service of God, and the promises; of whom are the fathers and from whom, according to the flesh, Christ came, who is over all, the eternally blessed God. Amen"* (NKJV). Through the Jews, we have the very roots and foundations of our faith.

As you're about to see, God loves Israel, Jerusalem, and the Jewish people. And when we align ourselves with blessing Israel, we align our lives with God's Word, His promises, and His plans. In other words, when you set your life to bless Israel, you will see God's blessing upon your life.

The Bible says that God is zealous for Zion with great zeal. It also says that He calls the Jewish people the apple of His eye. It says that His eyes are ever toward Jerusalem and, one day, Jesus Christ will return to Earth on the Mount of Olives. As the truths you'll find on the pages that follow reveal, there is simply no way to disconnect Israel from God and God from Israel.

Romans 9–11 outlines God's yet unfulfilled plans for Israel. In other words, God has not rejected Israel, and He has not replaced Israel. They are not cast away, and they remain the seed of Abraham. God still has a plan to make the riches of His glory known. In Romans 10:1, Paul wrote, *"Brethren, my heart's desire and prayer to God for Israel is that they may be saved"* (NKJV).

The biblical fact remains that God loves Israel. And He has established an everlasting covenant with them. He is mindful of Israel, and He has promised good things to them. In Jeremiah 31:3–6 (NKJV), we see a glimpse of His affections for Israel:

> *The* LORD *has appeared of old to me, saying: "Yes, I have* **loved you with an everlasting love**; *therefore with lovingkindness I have drawn you. Again* **I will build you**, *and you shall be rebuilt, O virgin of Israel! You shall again be adorned with your tambourines, and shall go forth in the dances of those who rejoice.* **You shall yet plant vines on the mountains of Samaria**; *the planters shall plant and eat them as ordinary food. For there shall be a day when the watchmen will cry on Mount Ephraim, 'Arise, and let us go up to Zion, to the* LORD *our God.'"*
>
> (emphasis added)

Get ready to discover that God cares about Israel and the Jewish people. And why you should, too. In my decades of walking with God, I've learned that when I become passionate about something that God is passionate about, I begin to see the blessings of those who live near to God's heart come about in my life.

I want that for you, too.

***"At the same time,"** **says the Lord,** "I will be the God of all the families of Israel, and they shall be My people.* ... Israel, when I went to give him rest." The Lord has appeared of old to me, saying: "Yes, I have loved you with an everlasting love; therefore with lovingkindness I have drawn you. Again I will build you, and you shall be rebuilt, O virgin of Israel!"

Jeremiah 31:1–4 (NKJV)

A
Biblical
Principle

In Blessing
I Will Bless You

In blessing I will bless thee, and in multiplying I will multiply thy seed as the stars of the heaven, and as the sand which is upon the sea shore; and thy seed shall possess the gate of his enemies; and in thy seed shall all the nations of the earth be blessed; because thou hast obeyed my voice.
Genesis 22:17–18 (KJV)

As a Christian, one of the most impactful decisions you can make is to commit to blessing Israel. God's purposes for Israel reach higher and further than much of the world can understand. For centuries, nations have arisen to try to destroy the Jewish people. Powerful armies and mighty people have tried to extinguish them, yet all these faded into the history books. But the *Nefesh Yehudi*, the Jewish spirit, remains because God divinely decreed it to be so.

Israel's story on the earth is intimately connected to God's purposes. God made an everlasting covenant to the Jewish people in the Old Testament. And throughout the New Testament and unto today, God's Word and His promises endure. That's why it is vital to support Israel.

If you want to know one of Heaven's keys to being blessed and to seeing the favor and the hand of God on your life, open your Bible and begin to study how God feels about Israel.

As you connect your own heart with Israel, you will begin to see supernatural increases of blessing, favor, and grace on everything your hand touches. Why? Because you aligned your heart and life with what God was already doing. When you begin to favor what God favors, and when you begin to bless what God has blessed, the blessings of God will find you. The favor of God will come on you in a magnificent way.

And as you study the Scriptures, you will discover that the city of Jerusalem often serves as a prophetic

***God made an everlasting covenant* to the Jewish people in the Old Testament.** And throughout the New Testament and unto today, God's Word and His promises endure. That's why it is vital to support Israel.

symbol for the nation of Israel as a whole and the Jewish people in general. What I have found is that there seems to be no limit to what God will do for those who connect themselves, their businesses, their homes, their families, and the work of their hands to the nation of Israel and to the beautiful city of Jerusalem.

God loves Jerusalem. In 2 Kings 21:4, He said, *"In Jerusalem I will put My name"* (NKJV). God is passionate about Jerusalem, about Israel, and about the Jewish people. It has, is, and will always be a big deal to Him.

This is the outworking of the promise God made to Abraham in Genesis 12:3. A promise that He would bless those who bless His nation, Israel. There, God told Abraham that He would bless him and his descendants.

And God is true to His Word! That promise is as active today as the day He made it. God will supernaturally bless and favor those who practically bless and favor what His hand, Word, and purpose are connected to.

It's important to never lose sight of the fact that Jesus is a Jewish Savior. In Revelation 5:5 we are reminded of Jesus' lineage. John wrote, *"But one of the elders said to me, 'Do not weep. Behold, the Lion of the tribe of Judah, the Root of David, has prevailed to open the scroll and to loose its seven seals'"* (NKJV). Jesus is of the tribe of Judah—eternally.

The word Judah is the word from which we get the word Jew. And not only was Jesus a Jew, but He still is a Jew. Our Messiah, our Savior, our Redeemer is Jewish. The first verses of the New Testament, Matthew 1:1–17, begin by tracing Jesus' Jewish lineage from Abraham to King David to Joseph the husband of Mary, of whom was born Jesus who is the Christ.

In John 4, we read the story of Jesus meeting the Samaritan woman at the well. And as He was talking with her, He made an amazing, astonishing, stunning statement. He said, *"Salvation is of the Jews"* (v. 22, NKJV).

Those five breathtaking words are New Testament. They are in your Bible today, printed in red, because Jesus Himself said them. It's an incredible concept that is forgotten in most pulpits today: no Jews, no salvation. We must always remember that salvation is of the Jews.

Jesus was saying that it was the Jewish people who were the physical conduit to bring the Messiah to the earth. Our entire spiritual inheritance is linked back to this. All of the blessings in your life and everything you have spiritually as an inheritance come back to the Jewish people, the city of Jerusalem, and the Holy Land of Israel.

Without the Jewish people, there would be no prophets, there would be no Old Testament, and there would be no patriarchs of the faith in Abraham, Isaac, and Jacob. There would be no apostles or New Testament because Jesus' disciples and those who wrote the Scriptures (except perhaps Luke) were Jewish.

All of the spiritual blessings you enjoy were wrapped up in the nation of Israel and the Jewish people. God has never taken His hand off of the Jewish people. So when you stand for Israel, pray for Israel, support Israel, and begin to bless Israel—you connect your life to an increased measure of God's blessing.

It's one of the most important lessons: if you want God's blessing on your life, bless what God has blessed. If you want God's favor on your life, favor who God has favored, and God's favor will come on you as well.

It's one of the most important lessons: if you want God's blessing on your life, bless what God has blessed.

Questions for Thought, Prayer, and Action:

- Since "salvation is of the Jews," what should be my heart's attitude toward them?

- What can I do to be a blessing to Israel and the Jewish people?

_____
_____
_____
_____
_____
_____
_____
_____
_____
_____
_____

A Divine Plan

Brethren, my heart's desire and prayer to God for Israel is that they may be saved.
Romans 10:1 (NKJV)

Romans chapters 9–11 contain the apostle Paul's most thorough explanation of God's plans and heart for the Jewish people. The truth about God's love for Israel is what motivated Paul's statement in the verse above.

When we look at the Word of God as a whole, we see that it is absolutely appropriate to support Israel and to pray for Israel. Our hearts should mirror Paul's. That means making up our minds that we're going to stand on the Word of God as we stand with

Israel. I want to challenge you to do that in faith and then watch what God does in you and for you.

Israel is a unique nation more than any other nation in the history of the world. And I've personally discovered that blessing comes to your life when you begin to honor and align your heart with what the Scriptures say about Israel.

It's important to understand that God is still connected to Israel. When Jesus came to earth, He came through the Jewish people. His entire heritage and line is through the Jewish people, and He is still Jewish in Heaven. He eternally remains the Lion of the tribe of Judah.

We worship a Jewish Savior and have pledged allegiance to a Jewish Messiah. As believers, we should honor and bless our Jewish brothers and sisters today. Salvation for the world came through the Jewish people and all our spiritual blessings are connected back to them.

Paul put it this way: *"They were pleased to do it, and indeed they owe it to them. For if the Gentiles have come to share in their spiritual blessings, they ought also to be of service to them in material blessings"* (Romans 15:27, ESV). That is a specific biblical exhortation for believers—to seek to tangibly bless Israel.

***Salvation for the world* came through the Jewish people** and all our spiritual blessings are connected back to them.

Questions for Thought, Prayer, and Action:

- Since, as a Christian, you have come to share in the spiritual blessings of Israel, how can you "be of service to them"?

_____
_____
_____
_____
_____
_____
_____
_____
_____
_____
_____
_____
_____
_____
_____

The Firstfruits are Holy

But if some of the branches were broken off, and you, although a wild olive shoot, were grafted in among the others and now share in the nourishing root of the olive tree, do not be arrogant toward the branches. If you are, remember it is not you who support the root, but the root that supports you.
Romans 11:17–18 (ESV)

As we've seen, Romans chapters 9–11 are a treatise on how believers are to view Israel and the Jewish people. If you have ever wondered what Israel means to God or what God's plan is for Israel, spend time in these chapters.

Romans reminds us of the incredible grace and sovereignty of God in His plan of salvation. This scripture speaks directly to the gentile believers, reminding them of their place in God's redemptive story. It is also an exhortation on the importance of humility and gratitude.

When the apostle Paul wrote, *"It is not you who support the root, but the root that supports you,"* he was talking about the relationship between the Jewish people and the church. The promises of the old covenant were originally given to Israel. When Jesus came, He brokered a new covenant and made a way for the church to be "grafted in" to God's promises.

He was saying it's not right for "grafted in branches" (the church) to become arrogant toward "original branches" (the Jews). And in Romans 11:1, Paul says, *"Has God cast away His people? Certainly not!"* (NKJV). God has not cast away the Jews, He is not done with Israel, and He has not replaced the Jewish people with the church.

Both the Jewish people and the church have distinctive roles in God's plan. In Romans 9, Paul writes of his kinsmen, Israel, that they hold a critically important role. For it is they *"to whom pertain the*

***Both* the Jewish people and the church** have distinctive roles in God's plan.

adoption, the glory, the covenants, the giving of the law, the service of God, and the promises; of whom are the fathers and from whom, according to the flesh, Christ came, who is over all, the eternally blessed God" (vv. 4–5, NKJV).

The Bible was given to mankind through the Jewish people. The story of how God related to humanity for thousands of years and the prophetic promises of the second coming of Christ have all come to us through the Jewish people.

Before Jesus was born, the Jews were the *only* nation on earth who were looking to the day when the Messiah, the Savior of the world, would come. And we must never forget nor diminish the importance that it was through a Jewish line that Jesus of Nazareth was born.

The bedrock of our faith as believers as laid out in the New Testament—stands on the firm foundation of God's faithful Word that He established through the Old Testament. The very roots of Christianity are found in the Jewish people and the nation of Israel.

God's dealing with mankind is a greater and grander story than we comprehend. There are thousands upon thousands of cross-references that intertwine the Holy Scriptures from Genesis to Malachi and from Matthew to Revelation. The Bible is one story, authored by one God, centered around one Savior: Jesus the Christ.

In Deuteronomy 7:6, Moses wrote, *"For you are a people holy to the LORD your God. The LORD your God has chosen you to be a people for his treasured possession, out of all the peoples who are on the face of the earth"* (ESV). And we know that Moses was talking about natural Israel.

But you and I, through Jesus Christ, have been grafted in, and now by grace through faith, we can claim the promises that God endowed to natural Israel because the church has become spiritual Israel.

Peter echoed Moses when he wrote, *"You are a chosen race, a royal priesthood, a holy nation, a people for his own possession"* (1 Peter 2:9, ESV). But it is not a replacement of one for the other. There is a difference between natural and spiritual Israel.

We get a glimpse of this in Romans 11:11–12 when Paul wrote, *"I say then, have they stumbled that they should fall? Certainly not! But through their fall, to provoke them to jealousy, salvation has come to the Gentiles. Now if their fall is riches for the world, and their failure riches for the Gentiles, how much more their fullness!"* (NKJV).

Therefore, there is a distinction of two roles—that of the Jews and that of the gentiles who believe in Christ. And if the blessing of salvation came to the gentiles—to provoke the Jews to jealousy, what will

***And you*, although a wild olive shoot,** were grafted in among the others.

Romans 11:17 (ESV)

happen if all Israel is saved? The "jealousy" Paul is referring to is that which would lead the Jews to desire what the gentiles received through faith—the blessing of salvation through Jesus. Paul uses the imagery of an olive tree to illustrate God's relationship with Israel and the rest of the world. The olive tree represents the rich heritage and covenant promises He gave to Israel.

When he wrote, *"If some of the branches were broken off,"* he is referring to Jews who did not believe in Jesus as the prophesied Messiah of Israel. But Paul continues and speaks to the gentile believers: *"And you, although a wild olive shoot, were grafted in among the others."* So, God is able to graft in believers in Jesus to the nourishing root of the heritage of Israel through faith.

If it was possible for God to graft in the "wild" branches (we gentiles) by faith, how much more appropriate is it for the natural branches (Jewish non-believers) to be grafted in when faith comes?

What a beautiful picture of God's redemptive love and grace. He chose to include us in His family and allows us to partake in the blessings and promises originally given to Israel.

We are adopted in and can now claim our rich spiritual inheritance in Christ as sons and daughters of God. But it is vital to keep in mind that this was only possible because of Israel—God's original olive tree into which we've been grafted.

Our faith is deeply connected to the history and promises of Israel. And it is important (as believers) to stand in solidarity with the Jewish people. When we do, we align ourselves with God's heart and His purposes. And we continue to look toward the day when *"**all Israel will be saved**, as it is written: 'The Deliverer will come out of Zion, and He will turn away ungodliness from Jacob; for this is My covenant with them; when I take away their sins'"* (Romans 11:26–27, NKJV).

Questions for Thought, Prayer, and Action:

- Are there portions of my heart or mind in which I am being "arrogant" toward Israel or the Jewish people?

- How can I turn my heart toward a posture of gratitude for Israel and the Jewish people? And in what ways can I give expression to that gratitude?

_____
_____
_____
_____
_____
_____
_____
_____
_____

Zealous for Zion

This is what the Lord *Almighty says: "I am very jealous for Zion; I am burning with jealousy for her."*
Zechariah 8:2 (NIV)

"Zion" is one of several biblical, prophetic names for Jerusalem. It was on "Mount Zion" that Abraham prepared to sacrifice his miracle son, Isaac, out of obedience born of faith.

It is there that God provided a substitute sacrifice, a ram, so Isaac could be spared. This was a powerful Old Testament type that pointed to the reality that one day God would provide His only Son as a substitute sacrifice for all mankind.

On this same hill, David eventually established his capital, Jerusalem. And there, David's son Solomon built the First Temple as an ongoing habitation for God's presence dwelling among His people, Israel.

It's hard to overstate the importance of Mount Zion in Israel's history. Or in God's plan of redemption. So we shouldn't be surprised when God says He is "very jealous" for Zion, that is, Jerusalem, as we see in the above prophecy by Zechariah. We get another glimpse of Jerusalem's importance to God in the 137th Psalm.

Psalm 137:5–6 says, *"If I forget you, O Jerusalem, let my right hand forget its skill! Let my tongue stick to the roof of my mouth, if I do not remember you, if I do not set Jerusalem above my highest joy"* (ESV).

Psalm 137 is recorded in the Holy Scriptures. It reveals insight into the depth of how much God cares for Jerusalem. If God is zealous for Zion and loves Jerusalem, it ought to be on our hearts as well. It ought to be a part of our faith. It ought to be part of who we are as a people, as a church, and as believers.

These verses are really quite incredible. It's a remarkable thing that the psalmist would use such powerful imagery: *"Let my right hand forget its skill! Let my tongue stick to the roof of my mouth."* Jerusalem is a powerful and unusual place. It is a city unlike any other on the planet.

***If God is zealous for Zion* and loves Jerusalem,** it ought to be on our hearts as well. It ought to be part of our faith.

I also particularly want you to notice what the Scripture says about Israel. In 1 Chronicles 17:21, it says, *"Who is like **your people Israel**, the one nation on earth whom God went to redeem to be his people, making for yourself a name for great and awesome things"* (ESV, emphasis added). Israel is a special people to God.

Look closely at the wording. They are the *"one nation on earth whom God went to redeem to be his people."* Through great and mighty deeds, God delivered Israel from slavery in Egypt, He deeded the land of Israel to be their inheritance, and He revealed Himself as God through them.

Israel is a nation whom He loves for all time. The Jewish people remain as a nation on earth today because they belong to God Himself. He chose them, He made a way for them, and He still protects them.

God said they were the one nation out of all the nations that He chose. He also went even further and said that there was one city out of the cities on earth that He called His own. In 2 Chronicles 6:6 He said, *"I have chosen Jerusalem for my Name to be there, and I have chosen David to rule my people Israel"* (NIV).

Do not think lightly about Jerusalem. Mount Moriah in Jerusalem was the mountain Abraham climbed with Isaac to sacrifice to God. Golgotha in Jerusalem is where Jesus went to the cross and died for the world.

It was in Jerusalem where Jesus prayed in the garden of Gethsemane until His sweat became drops of blood. It was in Jerusalem where Jesus walked the Via Dolorosa, carrying the cross. And it was in Jerusalem where Jesus paid the final price of all iniquity, became the propitiation for our sin, and redeemed us back to God.

He preached in Jerusalem. He proclaimed the gospel in Jerusalem. He was arrested and beaten in the Roman Praetorium in Jerusalem. He was crucified in Jerusalem. Jerusalem is the only city, of all the cities in the world, that caught the blood of Jesus as it poured down from the cross.

And one day, Jesus will return to the Mount of Olives in Jerusalem (Zechariah 14:4). The mountain will split in two and the nations of the earth will see and know that Jesus Christ—no longer a babe in a manger, but now a risen and conquering King—will rule supreme forever and ever.

Jerusalem is important to God and ought to be important to you as well. As Christians, it is important to stand with natural Israel today. They face threats from every side and around the world. And according to Ezekiel 38, one day they will be invaded by enemies from the north.

Who will be a friend to the Jewish people?
Who will stand with them?

Ultimately, Jesus Christ will have the final victory. And when He comes, He will bring revival to Israel and to the nations of the world, unlike anything we have ever seen before. Until that day, who will be a friend to the Jewish people? Who will stand with them?

They are a people precious to God. May we have the courage to set our face like flint to reach out, to stand up, and to support the Jewish people. And may we bless our God by standing with Israel. Perhaps one day we might even earn the honor of those who bear the title "righteous among the gentiles."

Questions for Thought, Prayer, and Action:

- What are you passionate about? What does it mean to be passionate about what God is passionate about?

- What does it mean to stand with Israel as a believer?

_____
_____
_____
_____
_____
_____
_____
_____
_____
_____
_____

"*Thus says the LORD of hosts: 'I am zealous for Zion with great zeal;* with great fervor I am zealous for her.'"

Zechariah 8:2 (NKJV)

Everlasting Covenants

An Established Covenant

"I will establish My covenant between Me and you and your descendants after you in their generations, for an everlasting covenant, to be God to you and your descendants after you. Also I give to you and your descendants after you the land in which you are a stranger, all the land of Canaan, as an everlasting possession; and I will be their God."
Genesis 17:7–8 (NKJV)

The Bible says that God never changes (Malachi 3:6). It also says that the Word of God cannot be changed and that not even a jot or tittle will pass away.

The land of Israel and the Jewish people have always been important to God. They were on His heart thousands of years ago and they remain so forevermore. Israel matters today, both on the world stage and to every believer in Jesus Christ as Lord, because God cares about Israel. He is zealous for Zion!

He has always loved Israel, and He always will. Israel is a key theme throughout the Bible—from Genesis to Revelation. Over and over, God continues to make mention of the Jewish people, of Israel, and of Jerusalem throughout His Word. More than any other topic, Israel is referred to over and over.

Throughout history, God has communicated to the world through His people—Israel. They are a sign. They are a message. The very existence of Israel is a megaphone proclaiming that the God of the Bible is who He says He is. God has never changed. He made a covenant to them roughly 4,000 years ago through Abraham, and His Word still stands.

God's covenant with Abraham was and is irrevocable. He reaffirmed that covenant to Isaac and then once more to Jacob. As we've seen, God renamed Jacob "Israel" and extended those covenant promises to "Israel's seed"—in other words, all of Jacob's descendants—the Jews.

Israel's story is an unbroken thread of covenant with God that stretches back through the centuries.

Israel is a key theme throughout the Bible—from Genesis to Revelation. Over and over, God continues to make mention of the Jewish people, of Israel, and of Jerusalem throughout His Word.

In fact, you can follow that thread all the way back to the first book of the Bible. We looked at this passage in a previous entry:

> *Now the* LORD *had said to Abram: "Get out of your country, from your family and from your father's house, to a land that I will show you. I will make you a great nation; I will bless you and make your name great; and you shall be a blessing. I will bless those who bless you, and I will curse him who curses you; and in you all the families of the earth shall be blessed"* (Genesis 12:1–3, NKJV).

God also made it clear that His covenant would extend to Isaac:

> *Then God said: "No, Sarah your wife shall bear you a son, and you shall call his name Isaac; I will establish My covenant with him for an everlasting covenant, and with his descendants after him... But My covenant I will establish with Isaac, whom Sarah shall bear to you at this set time next year." Then He finished talking with him, and God went up from Abraham* (Genesis 17:19–22, NKJV).

And to Isaac's son, Jacob (Israel):

"I am the LORD God of Abraham your father and the God of Isaac; the land on which you lie I will give to you and your descendants. Also your descendants shall be as the dust of the earth; you shall spread abroad to the west and the east, to the north and the south; and in you and in your seed all the families of the earth shall be blessed. Behold, I am with you and will keep you wherever you go, and will bring you back to this land; for I will not leave you until I have done what I have spoken to you" (Genesis 28:13–15, NKJV).

The God "who so loved the world" chose Israel as the place to begin making Himself known to the world and to begin the process of restoring people to intimate fellowship with Himself. As a key part of the plan, God proclaimed an eternal covenant connected to a specific people in a specific land.

God has not replaced Israel (the land or the people). God has not rejected Israel. And God is in no way done with Israel. God never changes. His Word tells us that He is an unchanging God.

He is the same yesterday, today, and forever. Man may change, but God never does. And when God made a promise and a covenant to the Jewish people and canonized His promises in Scripture, He meant what He said.

Questions for Thought, Prayer, and Action:

- Aren't you glad God never changes where His faithfulness to His covenants and promises are concerned?

- Since God granted the "land" to Abraham, Isaac, and Jacob and their descendants for eternity, why would anyone who honors the Bible question the Jewish people's right to live there?

_____
_____
_____
_____
_____
_____
_____
_____
_____

The Apple of His Eye

*"Up, Zion! Escape, you who dwell with the daughter of Babylon." For thus says the L*ORD *of hosts: "He sent Me after glory, to the nations which plunder you; for he who touches you touches the apple of His eye."*
Zechariah 2:7–8 (NKJV)

In the Bible, there are many Hebrew idioms. An idiom is a saying such as, "He's sawing logs." Or "It's raining cats and dogs." Many of these are literally "lost in translation" when the Hebrew manuscripts are converted to English. But a few manage to make their way through to English. Such is the case in the verse above.

The phrase "the apple of His eye" is an ancient Hebrew idiom that suggests Israel is very special to God and that He is very protective of her as a nation. This verse is just one of many that reveals how much God loves Israel. He has always loved her, and He always will.

In both the Old and New Testaments, the Bible consistently talks about God's purposes and plans for the nation and her people. They are always on His mind. God's enemies know that. Which is why Israel will always be a focal point of controversy and conflict on the world stage.

Throughout history, the enemy has tried to destroy the Jews around the world. He's still trying. But they are God's chosen people, and He still has a plan for them. That leaves us, as believers, with an important decision to make.

What will we do with the Bible's clear proclamation of God's love for Israel? How will we respond when it becomes unpopular, and perhaps even personally costly, to stand with Israel? In a rising climate of antisemitism and hatred of Israel, will we pray for her, love her, and support her? In other words, will we join the Lord in saying what He expressed to Israel through the prophet Jeremiah:

The LORD has appeared of old to me, saying: "Yes, I have loved you with an everlasting love; therefore with lovingkindness I have drawn you. Again I will build you, and you shall be rebuilt, O virgin of Israel! You shall again be adorned with your tambourines, and shall go forth in the dances of those who rejoice. You shall yet plant vines on the mountains of Samaria; the planters shall plant and eat them as ordinary food. For there shall be a day when the watchmen will cry on Mount Ephraim, 'Arise, and let us go up to Zion, to the LORD our God.'"
Jeremiah 31:3–6 (NKJV)

As Christians, we are called of God to be a friend to Israel, to stand with Israel, and to support Israel—even when it's unpopular. And in this fallen, broken world, doing so will usually be unpopular.

Currently, we have a generation of believers in the body of Christ who are disconnected from their Jewish roots, disconnected from the fact that our Bible is a Jewish Bible, and disconnected from the understanding that our Savior is a Jewish Messiah.

My prayer is that God will open the eyes of an entire generation to see and understand the signif-

When you understand the reality of the power of God's specific choosing of Israel, it's a powerful thing. It's a biblical reality: God has chosen Israel for His glory, His purposes, and His plans.

icance of Israel in the Bible. And if we'll lean in and hear, there's a blessing connected to it.

The truth is, God sovereignly chose the land of Israel and called it holy. And God sovereignly chose the Jewish people as a special people for Himself. Israel is a nation that God created, God decreed, God loved, God called, God elected, and God is actively protecting today.

When you understand the reality of the power of God's specific *choosing* of Israel, it's a powerful thing. It's a biblical reality: God has chosen Israel for His glory, His purposes, and His plans. Because of this, Israel is under special protection.

The commander of the armies of Heaven guards this chosen nation and these chosen people. This is why, in the face of centuries of persecution and oppression, they still exist as a distinct people with a distinct culture. The hand of God has protected this nation in a mighty way.

The Jewish people are the apple of God's eye. To Him, they are a special people, and Israel is a special place. Both enjoy God's special protection.

Questions for Thought, Prayer, and Action:

- How will I respond when it becomes unpopular, and perhaps even personally costly, to stand with Israel?

- If God has vowed to protect Israel, why would it be important to live in a nation that seeks to do the same thing?

Israel in Prophecy

"You shall be My people, and I will be your God."
Jeremiah 30:22 (NKJV)

You're probably beginning to get the key point your Bible is making. Namely, that Israel is unique among the nations of the world. And the Jewish people are unlike any other people group on the planet. Their whole history, the history of their land, their origin story, the ways God sovereignly guided them, and His future plans for them—it's all revealed in the Bible and foretold through prophecy.

Your Bible contains 16 specific prophecies about the nation of Israel. To date, 13 of those have come to pass. It was foretold and prophesied that they would go into slavery in Egypt. And it was foretold that they would be delivered from that place of bondage carrying Egypt's wealth. And it happened just as God decreed.

It was prophesied that they would possess the land of Canaan. They did. It was also prophesied that they would turn to idolatry. They did. It was prophesied that God would establish a temple in Jerusalem and that happened, too. It was prophesied that the Babylonians would invade, that Nebuchadnezzar and his armies would destroy the temple, and a large portion of the nation would be carried off into captivity. I'm sure you can guess how that turned out.

Just over 400 years later, Jesus prophesied that Herod's Temple, the one that replaced Solomon's, would be destroyed as well. In fact, to the astonishment and horror of His listeners, Jesus foretold that it would be so completely demolished that not one stone would be left upon another. Forty years later, that happened under Titus of Rome.

It was prophesied that Israel would be exiled from their homeland and scattered among the nations for many generations. And they were. It was prophesied that they would be persecuted by the gentiles. And they were.

It was prophesied that God would one day regather the Jews from all nations, restoring them to the land

Israel is unique among the nations of the world. And the Jewish people are unlike any other people group on the planet.

of Israel. And in the aftermath of World War II and the Holocaust, that too began to be fulfilled.

Seeing 13 out of 16 key prophecies come to pass yields an 81% fulfillment of Scripture. This leaves only three left to be fulfilled. And each of those three carries massive significance.

When we hold a book that accurately prophesied 13 major historical events about a nation, we should pause, consider, and take very seriously any other prophecies concerning that nation.

The first prophecy of the remaining three predicts a gathering of all the nations to war against Israel. Today we are seeing the beginnings of that possibility in the news. The prophecy from the book of Ezekiel is that "Gog and Magog" will invade Israel from the north. Gog is generally ascribed to the modern nation of Russia, and Magog to Iran.

When Israel became a nation again on May 14th, 1948, it was a miracle more unlikely and more astonishing than even the deliverance from slavery in Egypt and the parting of the Red Sea. And yet God had decreed it would happen. Through the prophet Jeremiah, God said:

> *"'I will bring back from captivity My people Israel and Judah,' says the* Lord. *'And I will*

cause them to return to the land that I gave to their fathers, and they shall possess it.'"
Jeremiah 30:3 (NKJV)

Since the reestablishment of the state of Israel, millions of Jews have made "Aliyah," that is, they immigrated to the land of Israel from the nations in which they were born. And according to Jeremiah's prophecy, they will never be uprooted again.

And in Matthew 24, Jesus talks about what will happen before His return saying, *"This generation will certainly not pass away until all these things have happened"* (v. 34, NIV). The point is that the time is short, and the second coming of Jesus is at hand.

Now consider this: the lifespan of a generation is 70–80 years. And as I write these words, the nation of Israel is now more than 70 years old.

What the devil fears the most is the return of Jesus Christ. And the Jews must be in Jerusalem for Him to come back—the Jews must be in the Holy Land of Israel (Matthew 23:37–39). That's why Satan is stirring up the nations of the world to hate both Israel and the Jewish people.

Today, it's becoming almost like it was in the days leading up to World War II where anyone can say whatever they want against the Jews. Antisemitism is very much on the rise and widely accepted around the world. Why? Because for Jesus to come back to Earth, the Jews must be in Israel and be in Jerusalem. And Hell dreads the day of His return.

The very existence of the Jewish people serves as a beacon to the world, declaring the power and reliability of the Word of God. God is not finished with the Jewish people and God has great and mighty plans for Israel. One day, the words of Zechariah 12:10 (NKJV) will come true:

> *"I will pour on the house of David and on the inhabitants of Jerusalem the Spirit of grace and supplication; then they will look on Me whom they pierced. Yes, they will mourn for Him as one mourns for his only son, and grieve for Him as one grieves for a firstborn."*

They will look upon Jesus and, when they do, they will realize He is the Messiah. The blinders will fade, and the scales will come off, and they will see that Jesus is the one who was *"wounded for our transgressions, He was bruised for our iniquities; the chastisement for our peace was upon Him, and by His stripes we are healed"* (Isaiah 53:5, NKJV).

The pinnacle of Israel's prophetic destiny is just over the horizon. The second prophecy yet to be fulfilled is the revelation of the Messiah to the whole nation of Israel and, finally, the second coming of Christ to the Mount of Olives in Jerusalem.

So many pieces are already in place. Israel as a nation has been reborn. Jerusalem has been reestablished. And Jewish people are returning to the land from around the world. One day, Jesus will return to Jerusalem and, when He does, every eye will see Him as the foretold Messiah.

Questions for Thought, Prayer, and Action:

- If past prophecies concerning Israel have been faithfully fulfilled, shouldn't I put my full confidence in those that remain?

- If the spiritual roots of hatred for Israel and of Jewish people are satanic, how can I guard my heart against these evils?

A People, a Land, a Covenant

When the sun had set and darkness had fallen, a smoking firepot with a blazing torch appeared and passed between the pieces. On that day the LORD made a covenant with Abram and said, "To your descendants I give this land, from the Wadi of Egypt to the great river, the Euphrates—the land of the Kenites, Kenizzites, Kadmonites, Hittites, Perizzites, Rephaites, Amorites, Canaanites, Girgashites and Jebusites."

Genesis 15:17–21 (NIV)

Israel belongs to God. The nation and her people are His treasured possession. Why? Well, the truth is, God does what He pleases. And it pleased Him to establish Israel as His land and declare the Jews as His own. He made that clear in Exodus 6:7 when He said, *"I will take you to be my people, and I will be your God, and you shall know that I am the LORD your God, who has brought you out from under the burdens of the Egyptians"* (ESV).

Yes, God chose for Himself a specific people out of all the peoples on Earth to be His own. They were a small people—just 12 tribes descended from a Middle Eastern Bedouin. They were not a mighty people either—so they would always have to depend upon God to be their protector and provider. In Deuteronomy, Moses said to the Israelite people:

> *"For you are a people holy to the LORD your God. The LORD your God has chosen you to be a people for his treasured possession, out of all the peoples who are on the face of the earth. It was not because you were more in number than any other people* **that the LORD set his love on you and chose you**, *for you were the fewest of all peoples, but it is* **because the LORD loves you and is keeping the**

Yes, God chose for Himself a specific people out of all the peoples on Earth to be His own.

> *oath that he swore to your fathers, that the* LORD *has brought you out with a mighty hand and redeemed you from the house of slavery, from the hand of Pharaoh king of Egypt. Know therefore that the* LORD *your God is God, the faithful God who keeps covenant and steadfast love with those who love him and keep his commandments, to a thousand generations."*
> Deuteronomy 7:6–9 (ESV)

Through this one nation, God gave the world the greatest gifts ever given. Paul wrote about some of the glorious spiritual gifts that God gave to mankind through the Jewish people: *"Who are Israelites, to whom pertain the adoption, the glory, the covenants, the giving of the law, the service of God, and the promises; of whom are the fathers and from whom, according to the flesh, Christ came, who is over all, the eternally blessed God. Amen"* (Romans 9:4–5, NKJV).

In other words, through the Jewish people, God gave the world the Ten Commandments, monotheism, the Bible, and the Messiah. We know every writer of the Bible from Genesis to Revelation, apart from the Gospel of Luke, was written by a Jewish writer.

To the Jewish people, God gave the Abrahamic and Mosaic covenants, the Old and New Testaments, the temple worship, and the patriarchs of the faith. Through the Jews, God communicated exclusively to mankind for thousands of years.

And then, above all else, the greatest gift given to all mankind, the Savior of the world, Jesus Christ, came through the Jews.

The Jews are still God's special people on Earth—"chosen" to be His vehicle for bringing the Redeemer into the world. And although that mission was successfully completed 2,000 years ago, God is not finished using them to carry out His good plans and purposes.

God's plans for mankind have always been connected to Israel and the Jewish people. His words and His will concerning Israel will come to pass. Though the nations rage against Israel, God's purposes will prevail.

No matter the attack, no matter how much the world's tyrants assault the Jewish nation, they will not be destroyed or driven into the sea. God is by their side and they belong to Him. They will endure, and God Most High will reign forevermore over all the earth.

That is why we support Israel and trust her survival, not to man-made institutions and international efforts, but to the God of all peace. And to the King of kings and Lord of lords.

Questions for Thought, Prayer, and Action:

- How can you better align your prayers to God's will and heart for Israel?

- What does God's faithfulness to Israel through the centuries tell you about His faithfulness to you?

"Up, Zion! Escape, you who dwell with the daughter of Babylon." For thus says the Lord of hosts: "He sent Me after glory, to the nations which plunder you; for he who touches you touches the apple of His eye."

Zechariah 2:7–8 (NKJV)

Faith in Action

Pray for the Peace of Jerusalem

Pray for the peace of Jerusalem: "May they prosper who love you. Peace be within your walls, prosperity within your palaces." For the sake of my brethren and companions, I will now say, "Peace be within you." Because of the house of the LORD our God I will seek your good.

Psalm 122:6–9 (NKJV)

I will never get used to visiting the beautiful city of Jerusalem. It is arguably the most important city on the face of the Earth. And the most significant city in the long, twisted history of the world. The first mention of it in the Bible is found in Genesis 14, when Abraham encountered Melchizedek, the King of Salem. In Genesis 22, Abraham and Isaac climbed Mount Moriah, the hill in Jerusalem often called "Zion."

In 2 Samuel 5, King David conquered Jerusalem. He *"captured the stronghold of Zion, that is, the city of David"* (v. 7, NASB). And Jerusalem became the capital of Israel. It was in Jerusalem that both the First and Second Temples were built.

It was in Jerusalem that Jesus laid His life down as the sacrificial lamb of God. In Jerusalem, He carried the cross through the Via Dolorosa of the Old City and paid the penalty of sin upon Calvary. The ground of Jerusalem received the blood of Jesus, and one day Christ Himself will return to Jerusalem when He comes again.

When Jesus saw Jerusalem, He prophesied about a day to come. He declared something incredibly significant that must occur in Jerusalem. He said:

> *"Jerusalem, Jerusalem, you who kill the prophets and stone those sent to you, how often I have longed to gather your children together, as a hen gathers her chicks under her wings, and*

It was in Jerusalem that Jesus laid His life down as the sacrificial lamb of God.

you were not willing. Look, your house is left to you desolate. For I tell you, ***you will not see me again until you say****, 'Blessed is he who comes in the name of the Lord.'"*
Matthew 23:37–39 (NIV, emphasis added)

One day, Jerusalem will say those blessed words, *"Blessed is he who comes in the name of the Lord."* But until that day, we watch and pray and long for His return. The city of Jerusalem is incredibly important to God.

Psalm 122 gives us a clear call: pray for the peace of Jerusalem. It is the only city in the history of the world that has a direct command within the pages of sacred Scripture that exhorts believers to pray for her peace.

We aren't given a reason why the Bible tells us to pray for the peace of Jerusalem. But we do have the exhortation to do so. And that appeal and encouragement is followed by a blessing of prosperity and peace! It says, *"May they prosper who love you. Peace be within your walls, prosperity within your palaces."*

Jerusalem is holy to the Lord. There will be a day when every pot in Jerusalem and Judah are considered holy (Zechariah 14:21). And in Revelation 21:10, new Jerusalem is called holy. It is the chosen city from all the tribes of Israel (1 Kings 11:32), and it is the city where God has put His name (1 Kings 11:36).

Without a doubt, Jerusalem, the City of David, the ancestral homeland of the Jews, holds a special place in God's heart. It is the only city that God calls His home. Psalm 135:21 says, *"Praise be to the LORD from Zion, to him who dwells in Jerusalem. Praise the LORD"* (NIV). It is the only city of which God has set His name, His eyes, and His dwelling.

Incredibly, the name of Jerusalem is found over 800 times in the Bible. In the Gospels, Luke 6:45 says, *"The mouth speaks what the heart is full of"* (NIV). As God is the author of the Bible, out of the abundance of His heart, He made mention of Jerusalem hundreds of times over thousands of years.

Matthew 6:21 says, *"Where your treasure is, there your heart will be also"* (NASB). Similarly, your heart will also follow whatever you pray for. If you regularly pray for the peace of Jerusalem, your heart will grow in affection for Jerusalem. And when your heart grows like that, you begin to love something that God loves dearly, and you will draw nearer to Him.

God has a purpose for Jerusalem. He established Jerusalem as His very own city, and one day He will even prepare a new Jerusalem. It is a holy city because God chose it to be so, and it is the city where the tribes of the Lord will go up to give thanks to the name of the Lord (Psalm 122:4).

***If you regularly pray* for the peace of Jerusalem,** your heart will grow in affection for Jerusalem. And when your heart grows like that, you begin to love something that God loves dearly, and you will draw nearer to Him.

God put Psalm 122:6 in His Word for a reason. And when we pray for the peace of Jerusalem, we pray for peace to reign, for hearts to return to God, and one day, for Jesus Himself to return as the King of kings and the Prince of Peace.

Questions for Thought, Prayer, and Action:

- Open your Bible to Psalm 122 and ask the Lord, "What is Your heart for Jerusalem, the Jewish people, and Israel?"

- As you pray for Jerusalem's peace and safety, will you extend your faith to receive a blessing of supernatural prosperity and peace for yourself?

Holy to the Lord

For thou art an holy people unto the Lord thy God: the Lord thy God hath chosen thee to be a special people unto himself, above all people that are upon the face of the earth.
Deuteronomy 7:6 (KJV)

Since the days of Deuteronomy—the Lord has called Israel holy unto Himself. He has claimed the Jewish people as His people. He alone set them apart. Perhaps that's why the world has hated the Jews so much throughout history. Perhaps that is why the word *antisemitism* is in our dictionaries. If God has established His love for them for all time, the enemy would take the opposing stance.

It's really an amazing concept to ponder: God in Heaven has openly declared that a specific people would be holy—to be "set apart"—for Himself. It should make us take notice.

The courts of Heaven have decreed the Jews to be a "Chosen People," and the territory granted to Abraham roughly 4,000 years ago to be a "Holy Land." We should not take that lightly. Why? Because the Judge who rules over that heavenly court is holy. He is resplendent in glory, and none compares with Him. King David wrote:

> *"Who is like your people Israel—the one nation on earth that God went out to redeem as a people **for himself**, and to make a name **for himself**, and to perform great and awesome wonders by driving out nations and their gods from before your people, whom you redeemed from Egypt? **You have established your people Israel as your very own forever**, and you, L*ORD*, have become their God."*
> 2 Samuel 7:23–24 (NIV, emphasis added)

Yes, Israel is holy to the Lord (Jeremiah 2:3), and God still has a plan for His special people. If that

***God in Heaven* has openly declared** that a specific people would be holy—to be "set apart"—for Himself.

were not so, Israel as a people would have faded into the pages of history long ago. Too many nations, empires, and armies have tried to eliminate the Jews from planet Earth. Each one powerful and mighty in its time. But it is they, not the Jews, who have disappeared.

Where are the Assyrians, the Seleucids, the Ottomans, or the Byzantines? Where are the Babylonians or the Roman legions? The power of the Persian empire during the time of Queen Esther has been broken. The might of the Third Reich is no more. Every nation, empire, and army that has come against the Jews, though they prevailed for a time, have passed away. Why? Because the Jews belong to God.

It's a sign and a wonder to the world that everything the Jewish people have been through has not diminished them. They keep becoming stronger because God has made it clear that Israel is His land, Jerusalem is His city, and He gave them both to the Jewish people.

The Jewish people today are living and thriving in their ancestral and historic homeland of Israel. Hebrew is the lingua franca of the land, and the biblical shekel is the modern-day currency. Orthodox Jews even still adhere to the feasts that God prescribed in the days of the Old Testament... *thousands* of years ago.

Yes—the invitation to God's great plan of salvation is through Jesus, who accomplished all at the cross. And yes—the church can now enjoy the benefits and blessings of being sons and daughters of God by grace through faith. But the Jews are on Earth for a reason. Israel exists for a reason. Jerusalem is a capital city in the center of the map for a reason.

One day, as Revelation tells us, Jesus will return to the Mount of Olives. One day, Jesus will enter the city of Jerusalem through the Golden Gate on the eastern wall of the city:

> *And in that day His feet will stand on the Mount of Olives, which faces Jerusalem on the east. And the Mount of Olives shall be split in two, from east to west, making a very large valley; half of the mountain shall move toward the north and half of it toward the south.*
> Zechariah 14:4 (NKJV)

A Muslim cemetery was established in front of the gate years ago. And in 1541, the gate was sealed by the Ottoman Sultan Suleiman for the sole purpose of trying to stop the Jewish Messiah from one day entering through. The Golden Gate is the only gate around modern Jerusalem that has been walled shut.

Jesus will return to the earth—
and Jerusalem plays a critical role.

Every other gate can be accessed by pilgrims from around the world, but in a futile attempt to block prophecy, that gate was sealed. But one day Jesus will return again. Nothing can thwart the plans and purposes of our great God.

The Jewish people as a nation are still holy to the Lord. And the last time Jesus came to Jerusalem, He said:

> *"O Jerusalem, Jerusalem, the one who kills the prophets and stones those who are sent to her! How often I wanted to gather your children together, as a hen gathers her chicks under her wings, but you were not willing! See! Your house is left to you desolate; for I say to you, you shall see Me no more till you say, 'Blessed is He who comes in the name of the L*ORD*!'"*
> Matthew 23:37–39 (NKJV)

Those verses are important because they give us a clue about what must first happen before Jerusalem sees Jesus again. The key phrase is when Jesus says, *"Blessed is He who comes in the name of the L*ORD*."*

Jesus will return to the earth—and Jerusalem plays a critical role. Therefore, the Jews had to survive throughout history. If the Spanish Inquisition wiped them out, or the Eastern European pogroms annihilated them, or any number of world powers succeeded in destroying the Jews, then there would be no Israel today.

And if there were no Israel, then there would be no Jerusalem, and if there were no Jerusalem, then how would Matthew 23:39 and Zechariah 14:4 be fulfilled? The Word of God must come to pass. All He has decreed will be fulfilled.

So, Israel exists. So, Jerusalem is alive. So, the Jewish people remain, to this day, holy to the Lord.

Questions for Thought, Prayer, and Action:

- What is God's plan for Israel, the Jewish people, and Jerusalem?

- What does it mean to be holy to the Lord?

I Will Not Forget You

Zion said, "The LORD *has abandoned me, and the* LORD *has forgotten me." "Can a woman forget her nursing child and have no compassion on the son of her womb? Even these may forget, but I will not forget you. Behold, I have inscribed you on the palms of My hands; your walls are continually before Me."*
Isaiah 49:14–16 (NASB)

I've been traveling to the Holy Land of Israel for roughly 30 years. And in the last few years, something powerful has shifted in my heart and spirit regarding Israel. In the midst of traveling there, I've tried to get my mind around it.

I feel as if I've always loved the nation of Israel, loved the Holy Land, and loved the Jewish people. But now... more than ever. Why do I feel such a connection to Israel? Why has the Lord laid the Jewish people so powerfully on my heart in this season? It's almost as though He has laid a measure of His love for His people on me—to sense or grasp His love for Israel.

Without a doubt, Israel is a special people. The nation carries a special purpose. And she operates and exists under special, divine protection. In each of Israel's wars, we find miraculous stories that can only be attributed to supernatural intervention. Stories of missiles diverting from cities, soldiers saved from ambush, and countless other testimonies of supernatural phenomena that resulted in victory for Israel.

God will never forget Zion. He Himself said, *"I have inscribed you on the palms of My hands; your walls are continually before Me."* It's significant to take note that this verse is talking specifically about the city of Jerusalem.

Jerusalem is the city where the Lord said, *"My house will be called a house of prayer for all the peoples"* (Isaiah 56:7, NASB). And God declared it is where He has set His name. It is the city to which King David brought the ark of the covenant. And it is the city where King Solomon built the Second Temple.

God will never forget Zion. He Himself said, "I have inscribed you on the palms of My hands; your walls are continually before Me."

Jerusalem will always be of utmost importance—to God, to Jews, and to Christians. The significance of Jerusalem to Christians will also always be connected to the Jewish people. Our Scriptures are shared. Our heritage is shared. Our history is shared.

We will always be intertwined with the Jewish people. It is an incredible thought to consider that the national history of Israel has now also become our spiritual legacy. And it is our duty to stand shoulder-to-shoulder with them.

The legal and national capital of Israel is Jerusalem. As Christians, Jerusalem is our spiritual capital. It is good and right for us as Christians to look to the peace of Jerusalem. God has not forgotten His city, and we must not either.

When God describes the love He has for Jerusalem, He describes it in terms we can all understand. One of the most powerful forces on the planet is a mother's love. And the imagery used in Isaiah 49:15 of God's affection for Zion is that of a mother who cannot forget her child.

We support Israel because God supports Israel. We stand with Israel because God stands with Israel. Supporting Israel is about coming into alignment with God's plans on the Earth.

It's about God's Word and God's covenant and God's promises. So we stand on the side of Israel because God in Heaven has proclaimed that they would be His people forever.

God has also chosen Jerusalem to be His very own. In 2 Chronicles 6:6, God said: *"I have chosen Jerusalem so that My name might be there, and I have chosen David to be over My people Israel"* (NASB).

Jerusalem is the City of David. It is the city of the great King (Psalm 48:2). It is the city where Jesus went to be the sacrificial Lamb and pay for the sins of the whole world. Jerusalem is the place of Calvary and where the cross stood.

One day, Jesus will return to the Earth to Jerusalem. When He does so, the Mount of Olives will split. Jerusalem is the only city of which God said He will make new. In Heaven for eternity, God will dwell in the new Jerusalem.

And in the book of Revelation, to the church in Philadelphia, Jesus said:

> *"The one who conquers, I will make him a pillar in the temple of my God. Never shall he go out of it, and I will write on him the name of my God, and the name of the city of my God, the new Jerusalem, which comes*

***Jerusalem is the only city* of which God said He will make new.** In Heaven for eternity, God will dwell in the new Jerusalem.

down from my God out of heaven, and my own new name."
Revelation 3:12 (ESV)

When Jesus came to Jerusalem before He went to the cross, He said that He longed to gather Jerusalem as a hen would gather her chicks under her wings. He also said that Jerusalem would not see Him again until it says, *"Blessed is He who comes in the name of the Lord!"* (Matthew 23:39, NKJV).

Jesus cared very much about Jerusalem. The Bible is clear: Israel is important to God, and Jerusalem is important to God. The Jews are Jesus' kinsmen, and we find God's words about Jerusalem, the Jewish people, and Israel over 2,000 times throughout the Bible.

Questions for Thought, Prayer, and Action:

- Do I need a better revelation of the ways I, as a believer, am entwined with the destiny of Israel?

- If Jesus cared about Jerusalem, shouldn't I?

Watchmen on the Wall

I have set watchmen on your walls, O Jerusalem; they shall never hold their peace day or night. You who make mention of the LORD, *do not keep silent, and give Him no rest till He establishes and till He makes Jerusalem a praise in the earth.*
                                     Isaiah 62:6–7 (NKJV)

God loves Jerusalem. It is a biblical principle. He loves Jerusalem so much that He wants watchmen on her walls. He wants prayer on behalf of Jerusalem. It is His city, and it is important to Him.

Jerusalem, the City of David and the ancestral home of the Jews, is close to God's heart. Psalm 122:6 exhorts us to pray for her peace—it is the only city in the history of the world to hold such an honor. God Himself is zealous for Zion and He has set His name there forever.

As believers, we would do well to love what God loves and be passionate about what He is passionate about. When God talks about Israel, the Jews, and Jerusalem, it is with eternal affection.

Malachi 3:6 tells us, *"For I the LORD do not change; therefore you, O children of Jacob, are not consumed"* (ESV). And Hebrews 13:8 says, *"Jesus Christ is the same yesterday, today, and forever"* (NKJV). God has always had a plan for Israel, and His promises to Israel do not change because God does not change. He is consistent and steadfast forever.

Who God was in the Old Testament, He is today. He made promises to protect and keep Israel, and those promises still stand. There is no waffling with God. He doesn't have second thoughts. His Word is true, and His plans are eternal.

If God said that the land of Israel would belong to the people of Israel, then forever it will. If God called the Jewish people His own, then they always will be. Numbers 23 says, *"God is not man, that he should lie, or a son of man, that he should change his mind. Has he said, and will he not do it? Or has he spoken, and will he not fulfill it?"* (v. 19, ESV).

We seek to support Israel, pray for Israel, bless Israel, and stand with Israel because Israel belongs to God. And as believers in Jesus Christ and followers of the God of Israel, we look to love what God loves, support what God supports, and bless who God blesses.

When you align your life with God's Word concerning Israel, you open the door for God's blessings over your life as well in a powerful way. When you make yourself a friend to God's people Israel, you open a new door to understanding God.

Israel is such a special place. I've been all over the world, and I can truly say there is no place that spiritually affects me as deeply as that land. And God has put His special people in His special land and set Jerusalem as the capital.

It's an amazing thing to consider, but at some point in history, God surveyed the whole Earth, and He found one spot, one piece of real estate, and He said, "That land is Mine." And then He took one city out of that land, and He called it holy. And then within that city, He zeroed in even further and called one mountain His holy hill.

***The most important spot* on the entire planet is Calvary.** Jerusalem was the physical location where the salvation of the whole world was won.

So out of all the places on Earth, God has a holy land, a holy city, and a holy hill. And on top of all that, He has a holy people set apart for Himself. The story of Abraham and Isaac climbing Mount Moriah is a beautiful picture and foreshadowing of Calvary.

Genesis 22:6 says, *"Abraham took the wood of the burnt offering and laid it on Isaac his son"* (NKJV). The wood was laid on the son's back and Isaac carried the wood to the place of sacrifice. In the same way, Jesus would one day carry the cross up the same mount to Golgotha (John 19:17).

When Abraham raised the knife, the Angel of the Lord stopped him. But when Jesus hung on the cross just outside the walls of Jerusalem, our heavenly Father did not stay the hand of those Roman soldiers.

He watched His Son bleed and die on that cross for my sins and yours. The most important spot on the entire planet is Calvary. Jerusalem was the physical location where the salvation of the whole world was won.

Because of what Jesus did in Jerusalem, John wrote: *"For God so loved the world that he gave his one and only Son, that whoever believes in him shall not perish but have eternal life"* (John 3:16, NIV).

Israel is a special place. Jerusalem is a special city. And the mount where Jesus paid for the sin of the world is priceless without measure. God has a plan for Jerusalem, and He has a plan for the nation of Israel. And one day Jesus Christ will rule the whole Earth as King and Lord from new Jerusalem.

Connect your life to what God is doing in Israel, in Jerusalem, and among the Jewish people. When our ministry started giving to the nation of Israel and the Jewish people, we went to another level. Something happened to our influence that I cannot even put into words.

God has blessed us because we made a concerted effort to bless His land, His city, and His people. You can do the same and set your life to be a blessing to Israel and the Jewish people.

Questions for Thought, Prayer, and Action:

- What would the Lord have you do on behalf of Jerusalem?

- Will you commit some time to praying for the peace of Jerusalem and record in a journal what God reveals to your heart?

Key Verses Concerning Israel

"I will bless those who bless you, and I will curse him who curses you; and in you all the families of the earth shall be blessed."
Genesis 12:3 (NKJV)

"Thus says the LORD of hosts: 'I am zealous for Zion with great zeal; with great fervor I am zealous for her.'"
Zechariah 8:2 (NKJV)

But Zion said, "The LORD has forsaken me, and my Lord has forgotten me." "Can a woman forget her nursing child, and not have compassion on the son of her womb? Surely they may forget, yet I will not forget you. See, I have inscribed you on the palms of My hands; your walls are continually before Me."
Isaiah 49:14–16 (NKJV)

Thus says the LORD, who gives the sun for light by day and the fixed order of the moon and the stars for light by night, who stirs up the sea so that its waves roar—the LORD of hosts is his name: "If this fixed order departs from before me, declares the LORD, then shall the offspring of Israel cease from being a nation before me forever."
Jeremiah 31:35–36 (ESV)

For I am not ashamed of the gospel, for it is the power of God for salvation to everyone who believes, to the Jew first and also to the Greek.
                                   Romans 1:16 (NASB)

For I could wish that I myself were accursed from Christ for my brethren, my countrymen according to the flesh, who are Israelites, to whom pertain the adoption, the glory, the covenants, the giving of the law, the service of God, and the promises; of whom are the fathers and from whom, according to the flesh, Christ came, who is over all, the eternally blessed God. Amen.
                                  Romans 9:3–5 (NKJV)

Brethren, my heart's desire and prayer to God for Israel is that they may be saved.
                                   Romans 10:1 (NKJV)

Again I ask: Did they stumble so as to fall beyond recovery? Not at all! Rather, because of their transgression, salvation has come to the Gentiles to make Israel envious. But if their transgression means riches for the world, and their loss means riches for the Gentiles, how much greater riches will their full inclusion bring!
                                Romans 11:11–12 (NIV)

For if the firstfruit is holy, the lump is also holy; and if the root is holy, so are the branches. And if some of the branches were broken off, and you, being a wild olive tree, were grafted in among them, and with them became a partaker of the root and fatness of the olive tree, do not boast against the branches. But if you do boast, remember that you do not support the root, but the root supports you.
Romans 11:16–18 (NKJV)

But Zion said, "The L<small>ORD</small> has forsaken me</mark>, and my Lord has forgotten me." "Can a woman forget her nursing child, and not have compassion on the son of her womb? Surely they may forget, yet I will not forget you. See, I have inscribed you on the palms of My hands; your walls are continually before Me."

Isaiah 49:14–16 (NKJV)

I pledge to pray for, support, and stand with Israel:

Signed:

_____

"Thus says the LORD of hosts:
'I am zealous for Zion with great zeal;
with great fervor I am zealous for her.'"
Zechariah 8:2 (NKJV)

Thus says the LORD***, who gives the sun for light by day*** and the fixed order of the moon and the stars for light by night, who stirs up the sea so that its waves roar—the LORD of hosts is his name: "If this fixed order departs from before me, declares the LORD, then shall the offspring of Israel cease from being a nation before me forever."

Jeremiah 31:35–36 (ESV)

JENTEZEN FRANKLIN

Notes

Notes

ABOUT PASTOR JENTEZEN

Jentezen Franklin is the senior pastor of Free Chapel, a multicampus church with a global reach. His messages influence generations through modern day technology and digital media, his televised broadcast, Kingdom Connection, and outreaches that put God's love and compassion into action. He has been honored with the Martin Luther King Jr. Mantle of Destiny Award for his work in racial reconciliation, the National Hispanic Christian Leadership Conference Micah Award, and the Jewish National Fund's Tree of Life Shalom Peace Award for his unwavering commitment to Israel.

Jentezen is also a *New York Times* bestselling author who speaks at conferences worldwide. He and his wife, Cherise, live in Gainesville, Georgia, and have five children and five grandchildren.

Jentezen Franklin Media Ministries aims to be a source of help and hope around the world. From comforting God's people in Israel, protecting the unborn, feeding the hungry, supporting hurting families, providing relief in areas struck by a natural disaster, to broadcasting the gospel—our mission is to share God's love and champion Jesus Christ to the nations!

To donate and learn more about the outreaches of Jentezen Franklin Media Ministries, go to:

JENTEZENFRANKLIN.ORG/OUTREACH

STAY CONNECTED:

JOIN US LIVE ON TV:

For broadcasting times and channel listings, go to:
JENTEZENFRANKLIN.ORG/TV-SCHEDULE